MY LIFE IN DOG YEARS

GARY PAULSEN

MY LIFE

in

Dog Years

with drawings by
RUTH WRIGHT PAULSEN

Thorndike Press • Waterville, Maine

Published in 2003 by arrangement with Random House
Children's Books, a division of Random House, Inc.

The tree indicium is a trademark of Thorndike Press.

The text of this Large Print edition is unabridged.
Other aspects of the book may vary from the original edition.

Set in 16 pt. Plantin.

Printed in the United States on permanent paper.

Library of Congress Cataloging-in-Publication Data

Paulsen, Gary.
    My life in dog years / Gary Paulsen ; with drawings by
Ruth Wright Paulsen.
        p. cm.
    Summary: The author describes some of the dogs that have
had special places in his life, including his first dog, Snowball,
in the Philippines; Dirk, who protected him from bullies; and
Cookie, who saved his life.
    ISBN 0-7862-2740-0 (lg. print : hc : alk. paper)
    ISBN 0-7862-6188-9 (lg. print : sc : alk. paper)
    1. Paulsen, Gary — Juvenile literature.   2. Authors,
American, — 20th century — Biography — Juvenile literature.
3. Dog owners — United States — Biography — Juvenile
literature.   4. Dogs — United States — Anecdotes — Juvenile
literature.   5. Large type books. [1. Paulsen, Gary.   2. Authors,
American.   3. Dogs.   4. Large type books.]   I. Paulsen, Ruth
Wright, ill.   II. Title.
PS3566.A834 Z47 2000
813'.54—dc21
    [B]   00-032608

MY LIFE IN DOG YEARS

COOKIE

A Dedication

Though I ran sled dogs for close to ten years, did some twenty-two thousand miles with them, this book is not about sled dogs or running them. They were truly wonderful and I have written of them in other books. This book is about other dogs in my life and other times. I am — I say this with some pride and not a little wonder — a "dog person." I make no excuses for unabashedly loving them — all of them, even some that have bitten me. I have always had dogs and will have dogs until I die. I have rescued dozens of dogs from pounds, always have five or six of them around me, and cannot imagine living without dogs. They are wonderful and, I think, mandatory for decent human life.

All that said, there are some dogs that are different, special in amazing ways. Josh is one, and you'll read about him later in this book. Cookie was another.

Cookie was my lead dog when I first started to run dogs, and she was also my lead dog in my first Iditarod sled dog race; she took me from Anchorage to Nome, Alaska, when most people — including me — thought I couldn't do it.

But she was more. She was a good friend, a kind of dogsister or dog-mother to me, and while I have written much of her in other places, she belongs in this book, too.

Cookie was given to me by a man who thought she was so sick she couldn't run any longer. She merely had worms, and when I wormed her she became a wonderful sled dog, and then a wonderful lead dog.

I did not set out to race dogs; I used them for work. I brought in wood with them, went to the Laundromat in town with them (it was grand to tie the dogs up to the parking meter and watch people jump as they walked by) and trapped with them.

In January of 1980 I was running a seventy-five-mile line, trapping beaver. I had previously trapped with a friend, but this year I was trapping alone, not the wisest thing to do, since there is some risk from bad ice or injuries and it's better to have a companion. I was alone when I made a mistake that nearly killed me.

The ice around beaver lodges is very dangerous. Beavers live in their lodges and come out of underwater tunnels to get food they have stored at the bottom of the river or pond through the summer, in the form of branches stuck down in the mud. Each time they come out they let air out of their noses and it goes up to make bubbles under the surface of the ice, and this, along with the beavers' rubbing their backs on the underside of the ice, keeps the ice very thin near a beaver lodge. It can be fifty below with two-foot-thick ice around the whole lake and the ice near the lodge might be less than a quarter inch thick.

I had parked the sled near a lodge and unpacked the gear needed to set a group of snares. Cookie was leading the work team of five dogs and they knew the procedure completely by this time. As soon as I stopped the sled and began to unpack they all lay down, curled their tails over their noses and went to sleep. The process could take two or three hours and they used the time to get rest.

A rope tied the cargo to the sled. I threw the rope across the ice to get it out of the way. One end was still tied to the sled. I took a step on the ice near the rope and went through and down like a stone.

You think there is time to react, that the ice will give way slowly and you'll be able to hang on to the edge, somehow able to struggle to safety. It's not that way at all. It's as if you were suddenly standing on air. The bottom drops out and you go down.

I was wearing heavy clothing and a parka. It gathered water like a sponge and took me down faster.

Two things saved me. One, as I went down my hand fell across the rope I had thrown across the ice, which was still tied to the sled.

Two, as I dropped I had time to yell — scream — and the last thing I saw as I went under was Cookie's head swinging up from sleeping and her eyes locking on mine as I went beneath the surface.

The truth is I shouldn't have lived. I have had several friends killed in just this manner — dropping through the ice while running dogs — and there wasn't much of a chance for me. The water was ten or twelve feet deep. I saw all the bubbles from my clothing going up to the surface and I tried to pull myself up on the rope. My hands slipped and I thought in a wild, mental scream of panic that this was how it would end.

Then the rope tightened. There was a large noose-knot on the end and it tightened and started pulling up and when the knot hit I grabbed and held and the dogs pulled me out of the hole and back up onto the ice. There was still very little time. I had a quart of white-gas stove fuel on the sled for emergencies and I threw it on a pine tree nearby and lit a match and set the whole tree on fire and, in the heat, got my clothes off and crawled into a sleeping bag. I stood inside it and held my clothes near the flame to dry them.

I would have died if not for Cookie.

She saw me drop, instantly analyzed the situation, got the team up — she must have jerked them to their feet — got them pulling, and they pulled me out.

That was January 1980. It is now 1997 as I write this, and everything that has happened in the last seventeen years — everything: Iditarods, published books, love, living, *life* — all of it, including this book, I owe to Cookie.

This book is dedicated to her memory.

SNOWBALL

The First Dog

Mother stood looking down at the puppy I was holding.

"This one," I said. "I want this one."

It was a little black female with a perfect white circle on its side and I clutched it close to my chest and saw only the puppy, me, and the endless possibilities.

I did not realize how impossible the situation happened to be:

I was just seven years old. We were in a mountain village in the Philippine Islands in 1946, where my mother and father had come on a sort of work-vacation-getaway trip. My father was in the army there and Mother and I had taken a troopship from San Francisco to be with him.

The dog represented a problem in more ways than one. We lived in strictly controlled base housing, such as it was, and Mother wasn't sure if dogs were allowed. But that was just for openers.

The village we were visiting raised dogs for food. I had just — to my utter seven-year-old horror — watched them strangle a dog for cooking. I grabbed the puppy thinking only to save it, but it was so cute that I immediately loved it and would not let it go. I had never had a dog before but there was absolutely no doubt in my mind that this dog, *this* dog, was meant for me.

The village headman who owned the dog was not eager to give it away and had reached to pull it back. Mother, who had been dickering over some carvings she wanted to buy, had seen the man reach for me and had come over like a tigress, ready to attack him, only to find that I would not let the puppy go.

"This one," I said again. "I want to save this one . . ."

"Save?" Mother asked.

"They eat them," I said.

17

"Dogs?"

I nodded. "I want to save this one and take it home."

She looked from me to the headman, back to me, then nodded and turned back to the headman. "How much?"

He stood mute.

"How many pesos for the puppy?"

He understood that and they started to haggle over price. My mother loved it and was in her element. I knew I'd won when she finally nodded, handed the headman some money, and motioned to the Jeep where my father and our bodyguard waited.

I do not remember much of the drive back down to the base. I sat in the back next to the bodyguard — a sergeant who had just fought through the Second World War and was completely bored with me, the puppy and life — and cuddled the dog.

The Jeep was open, with the top down, and conversation was nearly impossible at highway speed, but as we neared the base Father slowed down and Mother turned to me and smiled. "What are you naming her?"

I pointed at the white circle on the pup's side. "Snowball."

She nodded. "Perfect."

And so we became friends, Snowball and I, and more than friends.

It was a very strange time in my life. I was only seven and found myself dropped into a world that was in many ways insane. My mother and father were caught up in the whirl of being an officer and officer's wife involved in some way with the civilian government. This, coupled with the fact that they were getting a good start on their drinking careers, meant that I almost never saw them, and when I did they were usually not sober.

We had a servant named Rom, a young Filipino man, who took care of me when he could. But he had a family of his own, and I was left alone much of the time. Or left alone with Snowball.

The Philippines had been ravaged by the war and much of the islands was still in ruins. The people had been devastated, buildings bombed and blown to pieces, whole tracts of land pitted and scarred by battle. It was impossible to walk anywhere without stepping on empty cartridge cases or seeing some part of an exploded shell or mine. There were burned-out tanks and trucks everywhere, old Japanese fighter planes sitting on the ground, buildings blown in half and all too often a shallow grave or bulldozed trench with bodies in it.

This became my playground and Snowball became my guide.

We grew up together.

Snowball became an extension of me. I "went native," as they said then. I wore army shorts that were miles too big for me, an old army belt holding them up, no shirt, no cap. I sunburned constantly so I had a Band-Aid over my nose to keep it from peeling all the time, and I evolved into being Filipino.

Snowball grew tall in that first year, with a thin hound look, one ear flopped down, the other standing straight up, and her tail tightly curved over her back. I took to standing on one leg, my other foot cocked into the knee, one hand holding Snowball's back by the short fur. In many ways I think I became more dog than human.

I would see things — blown-apart buildings, old tanks, Jeeps upside down, rusting guns everywhere — but Snowball would *know* things. She would see the obvious outside way a thing looked, but then she would move to it and smell it and perhaps lick it and dig at it and look under it, and I took to doing the same things.

I would try to look inside what we were doing, follow Snowball's lead, and in doing this I found more and saw more than I ever could have alone.

We went everywhere, including many places where we were not supposed to be.

We found a cave in the jungle full of Japanese bodies — skeletons — and boxes of Japanese money and swords, and rats almost as big as Snowball.

We moved through places in Manila where people were so poor and hungry that a whole family lived under a single overturned Jeep and had only a handful of rice a day for six mouths. Still they offered us food — even a tiny bit for Snowball — and I took to "stealing" food from home and taking it to them and we would sit and talk their language, and eat rice and sardines with our fingers, and I would hear of their lives, Snowball next to me as we squatted in the dirt, and how the war had been for them.

We watched cockfights, where men put two roosters in a dusty ring and let them go at each other. Pesos flew around the pit while the men bet money on which rooster would win.

We moved outside of town, where the farmers wore conical hats and walked through rice paddies with huge water buffalo pulling wooden plows through the mud. Once, here, Snowball saved my life.

We were walking along a trail where the grass came down next to the dirt in tight clumps. I had gotten ahead of Snowball when she stopped to examine a pile of buffalo droppings. As always, I was barefoot, and I was shuffling along. Two steps ahead I saw a pretty colored ribbon lying along the trail. Another step closer and I saw it had moved. It wasn't a ribbon but a snake, one that — I was to learn later — was deadly. Some involuntary signal made me start to jump but I was too close. I was almost on the snake by that time. It was about to strike when a flash of black fur passed my leg and Snowball grabbed the snake just in back of the head and with a quick flick broke its neck.

It was all over in half a second.

I stood, shaking slightly, while Snowball made sure it was dead, threw it off to the side of the trail and continued on, stopping to look back, one ear up and the other down, her black face questioning, wanting to know why I wasn't coming. At last I regained some control and followed her.

We were in the Philippines two and a half years and I can't think of a day I spent without Snowball next to me. In many ways she became a kind of parent, watching out for me. When I slept she would crawl up beneath the mosquito netting at the foot of the bed and sleep with one part of her touching my foot or leg. The top of her head, her back, a paw — always she slept touching me, and when it came time to go back to the States I would not agree to go unless and until Mother made arrangements for Snowball to come with us. I made such a fuss that Mother and Father actually went through all the reams of paper it took to bring a dog from the Philippines to the United States.

But she did not come. Not two weeks before we were due to leave, a military truck swerved and hit her while she was walking next to me. She was killed instantly.

I remember standing, not believing she was dead, thinking how nothing would ever be right again, not ever, and how I would always, always miss her, and that is all true. Now, forty-nine years later while I write this, I can see her laughing tongue hanging out while she turns to beckon me on, see the white spot on her side, her tail curled tightly over her back as she turns and jauntily heads up the path ahead of me, and I miss her as much as if she'd just died yesterday.

Snowball.

IKE

A Good Friend

Much of my childhood I was alone. Family troubles — my parents were drunks — combined with a devastating shyness and a complete lack of social skills to ensure a life of solitude. This isolation was not natural, of course, especially for a child, and most of the time I was excruciatingly lonely. I sought friends whenever I could, but was rarely successful.

When I was very young these times of aloneness were spent making model airplanes, reading comic books or just daydreaming. But when I was twelve, living in a small town named Twin Forks in northern Minnesota, an uncle gave me a Remington .22 rifle he'd bought at a hardware store for ten dollars. I ran to the woods.

It is not somehow "politically correct" to hunt, and that is a shame for young boys. For me it was not only the opening into a world of wonder, it was salvation. I lived and breathed to hunt, to fish.

Two rivers ran out of town, one to the north and one to the east, and any day, hour or few minutes I could spare I would run these rivers. The first year I hunted mostly rabbits and ruffed grouse — feeding myself in the process. I scuffled along in old boots with a box of .22 long rifle cartridges in my pocket and the single-shot rifle in my hand. On my back was an old army surplus light pack I'd bought with money from setting pins at the local bowling alley. In the pack I had matches, usually a loaf of bread, salt and an old aluminum pot for boiling water.

There was great beauty in running the rivers, especially in the fall when the leaves were turning. The maples were red gold and filtered the sunlight so that you could almost taste the richness of the light, and before long I added a surplus army blanket, rolled up over the pack, and I would spend the nights out as well. During school — where I did badly — I would hunt in the evenings. But on Friday I was gone, and I would frequently spend the entire weekend alone in the woods.

The problem was that I was alone. I had not learned then to love solitude — as I do now — and the feeling of loneliness was visceral, palpable. I would see something beautiful — the sun through the leaves, a deer moving through the dappled light, the explosion of a grouse flying up through the leaves — and I would turn to point it out to somebody, turn to say, "Look . . ." and there would be no one there.

The second fall after I'd started living in and off the woods I decided to hunt ducks. Miles to the north were the great swamps and breeding grounds of literally millions of ducks and geese, and when the migratory flights started south the sky would seem to darken with them. The .22 rifle was not suited for ducks — was indeed illegal for them — so I saved my money setting pins and bought an old single-shot Browning twelve-gauge shotgun from a kid named Sonny. The gun had a long barrel and a full choke, and with number four shot seemed to reach out forever. I never became really good with it, but could hit now and then when the ducks were flying at the right angle. Duck hunting soon became my life.

I did not have decoys but I made some blinds six miles out of town where there were cattail swamps. I would walk out there in the dark, leaving the house at three in the morning, nestle into the blinds and wait for the morning flights to come in from the north. Usually I would get one or two ducks — once a goose — but some I wounded or didn't kill cleanly and they would get into the swamp grass and weeds in the water and I couldn't find them.

It was about then that I met Ike.

Ike was a great barrel-chested black Labrador that became one of the best friends I've ever had and was in all ways an equal; not a pet, not something to master, but an equal.

I had had other dogs. Snowball in the Philippines, then a cocker spaniel somebody gave me named Trina. They were sweet and dear and gave love the way only dogs can, with total acceptance, but Ike was the first dog

I'd ever known not as a pet but as a separate entity, a partner.

We met strangely enough. It was duck season and I was going hunting. I woke up at three and sneaked from the basement, where I stayed when my parents were drunk — which was all the time — up into the kitchen. Quietly I made two fried egg sandwiches at the stove. I wrapped them in cellophane (this was well before sandwich bags), folded them into a paper sack and put them in my pack along with a Thermos of hot coffee. Then I got my shotgun from the basement. I dumped a box of shells into the pockets of the old canvas coat I'd found in a trunk in the back of the coal room. I put on the knee-high rubber boots I'd bought at army surplus.

I walked from the apartment building four blocks to the railroad, crossed the tracks near the roundhouse yard, crossed the Eighth Street bridge and then dropped down to the riverbank and started walking along the water.

The river quickly left settled country and headed into woods, and in the dark — there was just the faintest touch of gray on the horizon — it was hard going. The brush pulled at my clothes and after a mile and a half the swamps became more prevalent so that I was wading in muck. I went to pull myself up the bank and walk where the ground was harder.

It had been raining, mixed with snow, and the mud on the bank was as slick as grease. I fell once in the darkness, got to my feet and scrabbled up the bank again, shotgun in one hand and grabbing at roots and shrubs with the other. I had just gained the top, brought my head up over the edge, when a part of the darkness detached itself, leaned close to my face and went:

"Woof."

It was that distinct — not "arf," nor "ruff," nor a growl, but the very defined sound of "woof."

I was so startled that I froze, mouth half open. Then I let go of the shrub and fell back down the mud incline. On the way down the thought hit me — bear. Something big and black, that sound — it had to be a bear. Then the word *gun*. I had a gun. I landed on my back and aimed up the bank, pulled the hammer back and put my finger on the trigger before I realized the gun wasn't loaded yet. I never loaded it while walking in the dark. I clawed at my pockets for shells, found one, broke open the gun and inserted a shell, slammed it shut and was going to aim again when something about the shape stopped me. (It was well it did — I had accidentally jammed the barrel of the shotgun full of mud when I fell. Had I pulled the trigger the shell would have blown up in my face.)

There was just enough of the dawn to show a silhouette. Whatever it was remained at the top of the bank. It was sitting there looking down at me and was the wrong shape and size for a bear. It was a big dog, a black dog. But it was a dog and it wasn't attacking.

I lowered the gun and wiped the

mud out of my eyes, stood and scraped mud off my clothes. I was furious, but not at the dog. There were other hunters who worked the river during duck season and some of them had dogs. I assumed that one of them was nearby and had let his animal run loose, scaring about ten years off my life.

"Who owns you?" I asked the shape. It didn't move or make any further sounds and I climbed the bank again and it moved back a few feet, then sat again.

"Hello!" I called into the woods around me. "I have your dog here!"

There was nobody.

"So you're a stray?" There were many stray dogs in town and some of them ran to the woods. It was bad when they did because they often formed packs and did terrible damage. In packs they were worse than wolves because they did not fear men the way wolves did and they tore livestock and some people to pieces.

But strays were shy and usually starved. This dog stayed near me and in the gathering light I could see that he was a Labrador and that he was well fed. His coat was thick and he had fat on his back and sides.

"Well," I said. "What do I do with you?"

This time his tail thumped twice and he pointedly looked at the gun, then back at my face, then down the side of the river to the water.

"You want to hunt?"

There, he knew that word. His tail hammered his sides and he stood, wiggling, and moved off along the river ahead of me.

I had never hunted with a dog before and did not know for certain what was expected of me. But I started to follow, thinking we might jump up a mallard or teal. Then I remembered my fall and the mud and that the gun was still loaded. I unloaded it and checked the bore and found the end packed with mud. It took me a minute to clean it out and reload it and before I'd finished he'd come back and sat four feet away, watching me quietly.

It was light enough now for me to see that he had a collar and a tag so he wasn't a stray. It must be some town dog, I thought, that had followed me. I held out my hand. "Come here . . ."

But he remained at a distance and

when it was obvious that I was ready to go he set off again. It was light enough now to shoot — light enough to see the front bead of the shotgun and a duck against the sky — so I kept the gun ready and we had not gone fifty yards when two mallards exploded out of some thick grass near the bank about twenty yards away and started up and across the river.

It was a classic shot. Mallards flying straight up to gain altitude before making off, backlit against a cold, cloudy October sky. I raised the gun, cocked it, aimed just above the right-hand duck to lead his flight and squeezed the trigger.

There was a crash and the recoil slammed me back. I was small and the gun was big and I usually had a bruise after firing it more than once.

But my aim was good and the right-hand duck seemed to break in the air, crumpled and fell into the water. I had shot ducks over the river before and the way to get them was to wait until the current brought the body to shore. Sometimes it took most of the morning, waiting for the slow-moving water to bring them in.

This time was different. With the smell of powder still in the air, almost before the duck finished falling, the dog was off the bank in a great leap, hit the water swimming, his shoulders pumping as he churned the surface and made a straight line to the dead duck. He took it in his mouth gently, turned and swam back, climbed the bank and put the duck by my right foot, then moved off a couple of feet and sat, looking at me.

I made sure the duck was dead, then picked it up and tied it to my belt with a string I carried for the purpose. The dog sat and watched me the whole time, waiting. It was fully light now and I moved to him, petted him — he let me but in a reserved way — and pulled his tag to the side so I could read it.

My name is Ike.

That's all it said. No address, no owner's name, just one short sentence.

"Well, Ike" — at this his tail wagged — "I'd like to thank you for bringing me the duck . . ."

And that was how it started, how I came to know Ike.

Duck season soon consumed me and I spent every morning walking and hunting the river. On school days

44

I would go out and come back just in time to get to classes and on the weekends I stayed out.

And every morning Ike was there. I'd come across the bridge, start down the river, and he'd be there, waiting. After a few mornings he'd let me pet him — I think he did it for me more than him — and by the end of the first week I was looking forward to seeing him. By the middle of the second week I felt as if we'd been hunting with each other forever.

And he knew hunting. Clearly somebody had trained him well. He moved quietly, sat in the blind with me without moving, watched the barrel of the gun to see which duck I was going to shoot at, and when I shot he would leap into the water. On those occasions when I missed — I think more often than not — he would watch the duck fly away, turn to me and give me a look of such uncompromising pity and scorn that I would feel compelled to apologize and make excuses.

"The wind moved the barrel," or "A drop of water hit my eye when I shot."

Of course, he did not believe me but would turn back, sitting there waiting for the next shot so I could absolve myself.

When the hunting was done he'd walk back with me to town, trotting alongside, until we arrived at the bridge. There he would stop and sit down and nothing I did would make him come farther. I tried waiting him out to see where he would go but when it was obvious that I wasn't going to leave he merely lay down and went to sleep, or turned and started back into the woods, looking back to see if we were going hunting again.

Once I left him, crossed the bridge and then hid in back of a building and watched. He stayed until I was out of sight and then turned and trotted north away from the bridge along the river. There were no houses in that direction, at least on the far side of the river, and I watched him until he disappeared into the woods. I was no wiser than I had been.

The rest of his life was a mystery and would remain so for thirty years. But when we were together we became fast friends, at least on my part.

I would cook an extra egg sandwich for Ike and when the flights weren't coming we would "talk." That is to say, I would talk, tell him all my troubles, and he would sit, his enormous head sometimes resting on my knee, his huge brown eyes looking up at me while I petted him and rattled on.

On the weekends when I stayed out, I would construct a lean-to and make a fire, and he would curl up on the edge of my blanket. Many mornings I would awaken to find him under the frost-covered blanket with me, sound asleep, my arm thrown over him, his breath rumbling against my side.

It seemed like there'd always been an Ike in my life and then one morning he wasn't there and I never saw him again. I tried to find him. I would wait for him in the mornings by the bridge, but he never showed again. I thought he might have gotten hit by a car, or his owners moved away. I mourned him and missed him. But I did not learn what happened to him for thirty years.

I grew and went into the crazy parts of life, army and those other mistakes a young man could make. I grew older and got back into dogs, this time sled dogs, and ran the Iditarod race across Alaska. After my first run I came back to Minnesota with slides of the race to show to all the people who had supported me. A sporting goods store had been one of my sponsors and I gave a public slide show of the race one evening.

There was an older man sitting in a wheelchair and I saw that when I told a story of how Cookie, my lead dog, had saved my life his eyes teared up and he nodded quietly.

When the event was over he wheeled up to me and shook my hands.

"I had a dog like your Cookie — a dog that saved my life."

"Oh — did you run sleds?"

He shook his head. "No. Not like that. I lived up in Twin Forks when I was young and was drafted to serve in the Korean War. I had a Labrador that I raised and hunted with, and left him when I went away. I was gone just under a year; I got wounded and lost the use of my legs. When I came back from the hospital he was waiting there and he spent the rest of his life by my side. I would have gone crazy without him. I'd sit for hours and talk to him and he would listen quietly . . . it was so sad.

He loved to hunt and I never hunted again." He faded off and his eyes were moist again. "I still miss him . . ."

I looked at him, then out the window of the sporting goods store. It was spring and the snow was melting outside but I was seeing fall and a boy and a Lab sitting in a duck blind. Twin Forks, he'd said — and the Korean War. The time was right, and the place, and the dog.

"Your dog," I said. "Was he named Ike?"

He smiled and nodded. "Why, yes — but how . . . did you know him?"

There was a soft spring rain starting and the window misted with it. That was why Ike had not come back. He had another job.

"Yes," I said, turning to him. "He was my friend. . . ."

DIRK

The Protector

For a time in my life I became a street kid. It would be nice to put it another way but what with the drinking at home and the difficulties it caused with my parents I couldn't live in the house.

I made a place for myself in the

basement by the furnace and hunted and fished in the woods around the small town. But I had other needs as well — clothes, food, school supplies — and they required money.

I was not afraid of work and spent most of my summers working on farms for two, three and finally five dollars a day. This gave me enough for school clothes, though never for enough clothes or the right kind; I was never cool or in. But during the school year I couldn't leave town to work the farms. I looked for odd jobs but most of them were taken by the boys who stayed in town through the summer. All the conventional jobs like working in the markets or at the drug-store were gone and all I could find was setting pins in the small bowling alley over the Four Clover Bar.

It had just six alleys and they were busy all the time — there were leagues each night from seven to eleven — but the pay for truly brutal work was only seven cents a line. There weren't many boys willing to do the work but with so few alleys, it was still very hard to earn much money. A dollar a night was not uncommon and three was outstanding.

To make up the difference I started selling newspapers in the bars at night. This kept me up and out late, and I often came home at midnight. But it added to my income so that I could stay above water.

Unfortunately it also put me in the streets at a time when there was what might be called a rough element. There weren't gangs then, not exactly, but there were groups of boys who more or less hung out together and got into trouble. They were the forerunners of the gangs we have now, but with some singular differences. They did not have firearms — but many carried switchblade knives.

These groups were predatory, and they hunted the streets at night.

I became their favorite target in this dark world. Had the town been larger I might have hidden from them, or found different routes. But there was only a small uptown section and it was impossible for me to avoid them. They would catch me walking a dark street and surround me and with threats and blows steal what money I had earned that night.

I tried fighting back but there were usually several of them. I couldn't win. Because I was from "the wrong side of the tracks" I didn't think I could go to the authorities. It all seemed hopeless.

And then I met Dirk.

The bowling alley was on a second floor and had a window in back of the pit area. When all the lanes were going, the heat from the pin lights made the temperature close to a hundred degrees. Outside the window a ladder led to the roof. One fall evening, instead of leaving work through the front door, I made my way out the window and up the ladder onto the roof. I hoped to find a new way home to escape the boys who waited for me. That night one of the league bowlers had bowled a perfect game — 300 — and in celebration had bought the pit boys hamburgers and Cokes. I had put the burger and Coke in a bag to take back to my basement. The bag had grease stains and smelled of toasted buns, and my mouth watered as I moved from the roof of the bowling alley to the flat roof over the hardware store, then down a fire escape that led to a dark alcove off an alley.

There was a black space beneath the stairs and as I reached the bottom and my foot hit the ground I heard a low growl. It was not loud, more a rumble that seemed to come from the earth and so full of menace that it stopped me cold, my foot frozen in midair.

I raised my foot and the growl stopped.

I lowered my foot and the growl came again. My foot went up and it stopped.

I stood there, trying to peer through the steps of the fire escape. For a time I couldn't see more than a dark shape crouched back in the gloom. There was a head and a back, and as my eyes became accustomed to the dark I could see that it had scraggly, scruffy hair and two eyes that glowed yellow.

We were at an impasse. I didn't want to climb up the ladder again but if I stepped to the ground it seemed likely I would be bitten. I hung there for a full minute before I thought of the hamburger. I could use it as a decoy and get away.

The problem was the hamburger smelled *so* good and I was *so* hungry.

I decided to give the beast under the stairs half a burger. I opened the sack, unwrapped the tinfoil and threw half the sandwich under the steps, then jumped down and ran for the end of the alley. I was just getting my stride, legs and arms pumping, pulling air with a heaving chest, when I rounded the corner and ran smack into the latest group of boys who were terrorizing me.

There were four of them, led by a thug — he and two of the others would ultimately land in prison — named, absurdly, "Happy" Santun.

Happy was built like an upright freezer and had just about half the intelligence but this time it was easy. I'd run right into him.

"Well — lookit here. He came to *us* this time. . . ."

Over the months I had developed a policy of flee or die — run as fast as I could to avoid the pain, and to hang on to my hard-earned money. Sometimes it worked, but most often they caught me.

This time, they already had me. I could have handed over the money, taken a few hits and been done with it, but something in me snapped and I hit Happy in the face with every ounce of strength in my puny body.

He brushed off the blow easily and I went down in a welter of blows and kicks from all four of them. I curled into a ball to protect what I could. I'd done this before, many times, and knew that they would stop sometime — although I suspected that because I'd hit Happy it might take longer than usual for them to get bored hitting me.

Instead there was some commotion that I didn't understand and the kicks stopped coming. There was a snarling growl that seemed to come from the bowels of the earth, followed by the sound of ripping cloth, screams, and then the fading slap of footsteps running away.

For another minute I remained curled up, then opened my eyes to find that I was alone.

But when I rolled over I saw the dog.

It was the one that had been beneath the stairs. Brindled, patches of hair gone, one ear folded over and the other standing straight and notched from fighting. He didn't seem to be any particular breed. Just big and rangy, right on the edge of ugly, though I would come to think of him as beautiful. He was Airedale crossed with hound crossed with alligator.

Alley dog. Big, tough, mean alley dog. As I watched he spit cloth — it looked like blue jeans — out of his mouth.

"You bit Happy, and sent them running?" I asked.

He growled, and I wasn't sure if it was with menace, but he didn't bare his teeth and didn't seem to want to attack me. Indeed, he had saved me.

"Why?" I asked. "What did I do to deserve . . . oh, the hamburger."

I swear, he pointedly looked at the bag with the second half of hamburger in it.

"You want more?"

He kept staring at the bag and I thought, *Well, he sure as heck deserves it.* I opened the sack and gave him the rest of it, which disappeared down his throat as if a hole had opened into the universe.

He looked at the bag.

"That's it," I said, brushing my hands together. "The whole thing."

A low growl.

"You can rip my head off — there still isn't any more hamburger." I removed the Coke and handed him the bag, which he took, held on the ground with one foot and deftly ripped open with his teeth.

"See? Nothing." I was up by this time and I started to walk away. "Thanks for the help. . . ."

He followed me. Not close, perhaps eight feet back, but matching my speed. It was now nearly midnight and I was tired and sore from setting pins and from the kicks that had landed on my back and sides.

"I don't have anything to eat at home but crackers and peanut butter and jelly," I told him. I kept some food in the basement of the apartment building, where I slept near the furnace.

He kept following and, truth be known, I didn't mind. I was still half scared of him but the memory of him spitting out bits of Happy's pants and the sound of the boys running off made me smile. When I arrived at the apartment house I held the main door open and he walked right in. I opened the basement door and he followed me down the steps into the furnace room.

I turned the light on and could see that my earlier judgment had been correct. He was scarred from fighting, skinny and flat sided and with patches of hair gone. His nails were worn down from scratching concrete.

"Dirk," I said. "I'll call you Dirk." I had been trying to read a detective novel and there was a tough guy in it named Dirk. "You look like somebody named Dirk."

And so we sat that first night. I had two boxes of Ritz crackers I'd hustled somewhere, a jar of peanut butter and another one of grape jelly, and a knife from the kitchen upstairs. I would smear a cracker, hand it to him — he took each one with great care and gentleness — and then eat one myself. We did this, back and forth, until both boxes were empty and my stomach was bulging; then I fell asleep on the old outdoor lounge I used for furniture.

The next day was a school day. I

woke up and found Dirk under the basement stairs, watching me. When I opened the door he trotted up the steps and outside — growling at me as he went past — and I started off to school.

He followed me at a distance, then stopped across the street when I went into the front of the school building. I thought I'd probably never see him again.

But he was waiting when I came out that afternoon, sitting across the street by a mailbox. I walked up to him.

"Hi, Dirk." I thought of petting him but when I reached a hand out he growled. "All right — no touching."

I turned and made my way toward the bowling alley. It was Friday and sometimes on Friday afternoon there were people who wanted to bowl early and I could pick up a dollar or two setting pins.

Dirk followed about four feet back — closer than before — and as I made my way along Second Street and came around the corner by Ecker's Drugstore I ran into Happy. He had only two of his cohorts with him and I don't think they had intended to do me harm, but I surprised them and Happy took a swing at me.

Dirk took him right in the middle. I mean bit him in the center of his stomach, hard, before Happy's fist could get to me. Happy screamed and doubled over and Dirk went around and ripped into his rear and kept tearing at it even as Happy and his two companions fled down the street.

It was absolutely great. Maybe one of the great moments in my life.

I had a bodyguard.

It was as close to having a live nuclear weapon as you can get. I cannot say we became friends. I touched him only once, when he wasn't looking — I petted him on the head and received a growl and a lifted lip for it. But we became constant companions. Dirk moved into the basement with me, and I gave him a hamburger every day and hustled up dog food for him and many nights we sat down there eating Ritz crackers and he watched me working on stick model airplanes.

He followed me to school, waited for me, followed me to the bowling alley, waited for me. He was with me everywhere I went, always back three or four feet, always with a soft growl, and to my great satisfaction every time he saw Happy — *every* time — Dirk would try to remove some part of his body with as much violence as possible.

He caused Happy and his mob to change their habits. They not only stopped hunting me but went out of their way to avoid me, or more specifically, Dirk. In fact after that winter and spring they never bothered me again, even after Dirk was gone.

Dirk came to a wonderful end. I always thought of him as a street dog — surely nobody owned him — and in the summer when I was hired to work on a farm four miles east of town I took him with me. We walked all the way out to the farm, Dirk four feet in back of me, and he would trot along beside the tractor when I plowed, now and then chasing the hundreds of seagulls that came for the worms the plow turned up.

The farmer, whose name was Olaf, was a bachelor and did not have a dog. I looked over once to see Dirk sitting next to Olaf while we ate some sandwiches and when Olaf reached out to pet him Dirk actually — this was the first time I'd seen it — wagged his tail.

He'd found a home.

I worked the whole summer there and when it came time to leave, Dirk remained sitting in the yard as I walked down the driveway. The next summer I had bought an old Dodge for twenty-five dollars and I drove out to Olaf's to say hello and saw Dirk out in a field with perhaps two hundred sheep. He wasn't herding them, or chasing them, but was just standing there, watching the flock.

"You have him with the sheep?" I asked Olaf.

He nodded. "Last year I lost forty-three to coyotes," he said. "This year not a one. He likes to guard things, doesn't he?"

I thought of Dirk chasing Happy down the street, and later spitting out bits of his pants, and I smiled. "Yeah, he sure does."

REX

The Farm Dog

They are all there in my memory, a host of them from farms I worked on when I was a boy. They all seemed to be some kind of collie cross with longish hair and bright eyes and all seemed to be named Rex or King or Spot or Lad or Jim.

They worked the farms. It is tempting to call them family dogs or family pets because they were that as well — something the small children could roll around with, something to love and be loved, something to greet in the morning. But they were more.

I cannot count the number of times I have been sitting in a truck waiting for a combine hopper to fill, a boy thirteen, fourteen years old on a hot August afternoon with an old collie dog sitting in the seat beside me.

You could talk to them and they would listen. I'd tell them of my dreams, my problems, girls — endless talk of girls — as I sat there in the hot sun chewing on a straw, ruffling a dog's ears and watching the combine rumble around the golden field.

They became in some way more

than another person could be, perfect companions, and it bothered me that I didn't know all of how they lived, only saw them at odd times during the day. One morning when we were rained out and couldn't work the fields I decided to follow the farm dog around through his day.

His name was Rex and he was a large collie type, slightly overweight, with a white ruff and thick gold hair matted here and there with burrs — all the colors smudged liberally with fresh, green cow manure he'd rolled in just that morning in back of the barn. (They love the smell of fresh manure on their backs and the sides of their necks.)

This particular farm had nine milk cows, three pigs, a pen of calves, a couple of palomino ponies for two daughters who would someday be old enough to ride them, a coop full of chickens and perhaps five hundred acres under cultivation.

I walked out in the morning after a quick cup of coffee and made my way to the barn with the farmer, a stooped man named Warren, to begin milking. There was already a light mist that would be rain, and as soon as we were out of the yard carrying buckets to the barn Rex was off like a shot into the haze in the direction of the pasture.

He did not need to be told but ran to where the cows were, went around them several times to form them up and with a couple of gentle nips got them heading for the barn. I have read somewhere that the reason dogs work stock is that the wolf in them is still strong and the herding instinct is a perversion of the hunting drive that moves wolves.

It sounds like a tidy theory, but having watched Rex and dogs like him work animals, I don't think it can be right. Every move they make is concerned with care for the animal they are herding, not with hunting, not with killing them. I have seen wolves course and kill and there is nothing similar about their actions.

Rex ran ahead of the cows, then behind, keeping them in a group and watching out for anything that could bother them.

When they reached the barn he stopped driving them and waited patiently for each cow — and they most decidedly did *not* hurry — to step into the barn and work her way to her stall before he would signal the next one in. All of this done without a word from Warren.

There was business in it, of course — it was work, and important — but there was affection as well. Rex obviously liked the cows and when Warren told me that Rex slept with them in the winter, curling up next to a cow in the barn to stay warm and cozy, I could see why when Rex looked at them it was with more than business in his eyes.

When the cows were all in their stalls and being milked, Rex went to the head of the barn and sat by the door, waiting. I was not certain what he was waiting for until Warren poured some milk into an old pail lid and put it down and the cats materialized from the loft and other parts of the barn and began to drink. I'd had no idea there were so many cats. They seemed to come from everywhere. Rex watched them eat and when one kitten kept getting pushed away from the crowded pan Rex used his nose to make a slot for the kitten and pushed it into place with another nudge.

He watched them until they had devoured the milk — a matter of moments — and then turned and left the barn, trotting out into the rain.

I followed him. He went to the pigpen and stood looking at the pigs for a moment. Then the calf pen, where he stopped. I know it sounds far-fetched, but he seemed to study each calf individually, or perhaps he was counting them. From there he went to the chicken coop.

Here he paused and turned. He

had seen me following him at a distance and he looked at me and wagged his tail and started for me. But I turned as if to walk back into the barn, and he returned to the chicken yard. I stopped behind a corner and watched him go around the wired-in yard several times as he studied the fence, looking for holes. When he was satisfied, he trotted to the corral that held the two ponies and when they were clearly all right he came back into the barn.

The whole route had taken ten minutes. He sat for a moment near the empty milk pan, then stood and walked up and down the barn several times, looking at each cow from the rear. That finished, he turned and went in front of them, walking back and forth in the narrow slot in front of the manger and studying each cow as she chewed on her hay.

It never really ended. I thought that with his rounds done, he would relax. Instead he started over: the pigpen, the calf pen, and this time he spent more time on the chicken yard, carefully smelling along the base of the wire at one side. At one point in particular he nosed the dirt, snuffling the mud slightly. When he returned to the barn I went to that spot and saw the fresh tracks of a skunk that must have tried to get into the pen during the night. (The next night Rex would catch the skunk trying to get to the chickens again and kill it in a battle that left the mauled body of the skunk by the granary and the entire barnyard so thick in stink it was hard to walk through it.)

Once more in the barn Rex sat for a moment. He was sitting there when I came in to help finish the chores. In a moment he moved to the wooden manger in front of the cows. This time he climbed the crude ladder to the hayloft, until his head was just up in the loft. He stood there for a moment, then went down the ladder, and up and down the line of cows one more time, front and rear, then outside to check the other stock . . .

He didn't stop his circling route until we were done with milking. Then he escorted the cows out of the barn — not pushing them but simply walking along with them — and took them back out to the pasture.

"He doesn't just leave them in back of the barn?" I asked Warren.

"Who — oh, the dog?" His wife had

told me the dog's name was Rex. I never heard Warren say his name. Just "the dog," but spoken in soft terms, with deep affection and care. Even when he called Rex, he simply said, "Come here, dog," always soft and gentle. "Oh no — he'll take them out to where the grass is good so they can graze. There's no grass in back of the barn."

"He knows that — to take them to grass?"

Warren looked at me. "Sure — why not?"

"But how could he know that? Did you teach him?"

Warren shook his head. "Not me — the cows. He watches the cows. They taught him."

I knew then, and I know now, people who would not be able to learn that. I was skeptical that a dog could learn such things — I was very young and had not yet known dogs like Josh and Cookie — but by the end of the day I would not have been surprised to hear that Rex had learned to read.

With milking done we went back to the house for a "quick bite" after breakfast of raw-fried potatoes, a bit of venison, rhubarb sauce and fresh rolls. Rex did not come in the house — he never came in — but Warren's wife, Emily, took him a plate of meat and potato scraps as he waited on the porch. I watched him through the kitchen window. He didn't relax. From where he sat on the porch he kept watching the farm-yard, the stock pens, the cows out in the pasture. I thought of pictures I'd seen of lions in Africa surveying the veld — his ruff made a wonderful mane — and he maintained control until the girls awakened and came out to play.

They were young — three and five — and when it rained they stayed mostly on the open porch, with forays into the yard for toys they'd left out. The minute they went outside they came under Rex's control. On the porch he sat near them, watching them play, sometimes reaching over with a paw to move a toy and laugh and wag his tail. When one of the girls left the porch he would move with her, staying always on the "outside" to contain her, and as soon as she'd picked up the toy she'd gone after, he would gently guide her back to the play area.

All day, or nearly all day, he stayed with the children. When the girls went in for lunch Rex took the time to patrol the yard again, and I noted that when one of the girls went near the pigpen — she was never closer than fifteen yards — Rex stopped her and used his shoulder to physically move her back to the house.

At intervals throughout the day he would take moments — never more than one or two minutes — to make a quick run of the yard and the stock to make sure it was all doing well, but the rest of the time he watched the children. He didn't just sit with them, or doze by them, or stand near them. He literally watched them. He played with them as well, but he was truly working the whole time and his eyes rarely left them.

"Isn't he a caution?" Emily said, noticing me watching Rex. "It's like having a nanny for them. When I'm gone visiting with them he stays with Warren and follows the tractor in the fields but anytime the girls are here he's with them. It's so nice. There are so many things to worry about on a farm."

It made a very full day. When we milked at night Rex ran for the cows, circled the yard and took care of all his business. When supper was done and it was getting dark I looked through the window expecting to see him sleeping, or at least lying down.

He was sitting on the porch, the evening sunlight and breeze catching his hair, his eyes open and calm, watching the yard, the pens and stock. While I looked he stood, trotted off around the yard one more time before dark, then came back to the porch to sit again, always at work.

CAESAR

The Giant

The dog was enormous.

We lived in a small cottage in the mountains of Colorado, where I worked in construction, mostly hitting my fingers with a hammer and making serious attempts at cutting something off my body with power saws while I tried to build houses during the day and write at night. I had been looking at the local consumer guide, called *The Shopper's Bulletin*, when I saw an ad:

EMERGENCY! AM LEAVING FOR HAWAII FOR A CAREER CHANGE. MUST FIND HOME FOR LOVING GREAT DANE NAMED CAESAR AS THEY WON'T ALLOW DOGS IN THE ISLANDS. PLEASE HELP!

All right — I know how it sounds. Nobody who lives in a small cottage in the mountains of Colorado with a wife and baby should probably even consider a pet, let alone a dog, let alone a large dog, let alone a *very* large dog — at least nobody with a brain larger than a walnut. But I had once been associated with a female Great Dane named Dad when I was in the army and had ever since had a warm place in my soul for them. The secondary force, the force that kicks in whenever I visit a dog pound, roared into my mind, the force that says, *If you don't take him, who will?* This drive has brought me dozens of dogs and cats, a few ducks, some geese, a half dozen guinea pigs, an ocelot, several horses, two cows, a litter of pigs (followed by more and more litters — my God, they are prolific), one hawk, a blue heron, a large lizard, some dozen or so turtles, a porcupine and God knows how many wounded birds; chipmunks, squirrels and one truly evil llama (am I the *only* person in the world who did not know they can spit dead level for about fifteen yards, hitting your eye every time?).

And so this man brought Caesar, who looked more like a *Tyrannosaurus rex* than a dog, into our small cottage.

His measurements were astounding. He stood forty-one inches at the front shoulder, his head a bit higher, and when he got up on his back legs and put his feet on my shoulders he could drip spit (his favorite hobby seemed to be disseminating spit and slobber) on top of my bald spot.

But size is relative. Had we seen him out in the open, say from half a mile away in the middle of a large field, he would have looked magnificent. Here, in a small room, he overwhelmed the furniture.

"Isn't he, you know," my wife said,

moving to a position of relative safety in back of the couch, "rather large?"

The man shook his head. "It's just because he's in here. Take him out for a run alongside the car and you won't even notice him. Why, just the other day I was talking to my girlfriend and she was saying how Caesar seemed to be getting smaller because he fit into her closet so well, kind of back in the dark" — he moved toward the door as he spoke — "where he likes to make a bed, out of the way back in the dark" — his hand was on the knob — "why, in a short time you won't even know he's here. . . ."

And he was gone. I won't say he ran, but by the time the door was latched he had his car started and was pulling out of the driveway.

It all happened so fast I don't think

the dog even knew he was gone. He sat for a moment, staring at me, then out the window; then he climbed on the couch, knocking over the coffee table, two end tables and a lamp. He used his paw to push the drapes aside and saw the car just as it was disappearing and he made a sound like a cross between the closing whistle at a major auto plant and how I imagined the hound of the Baskervilles would sound.

Then he climbed down, moved to the front door and sat.

Staring at the door.

Waiting.

"Well," I said, "that wasn't so bad, was it?"

My wife looked around at the wreckage — when he'd jumped down he'd put his weight on the back of the couch and tipped it over — and sighed. "What do you suppose happens when he has to go to the bathroom?"

It nearly became a moot point. For a time it didn't look as if he would live. I have never seen a dog grieve like Caesar.

His heart was truly broken. He sat by the door all that day and all that first night and when it was apparent his owner was not coming back right away, he lay down with his nose aimed at the door and waited.

Although he would drink a small amount of water, he would eat nothing. Great Danes are not fat in the best of times — all angles and bones — and within two days he looked positively emaciated. I tried everything. Special dog foods, cooked hamburger, raw liver, bits of bread with honey, fresh steak — he wouldn't touch any of it.

The third day I called a vet.

"Does he drink?"

"Barely."

"How long since he's had food?"

"Two, no, three days."

A long pause. "Well, if he's drinking he's not going to dehydrate. Give him a couple more days and if he doesn't eat then you'll have to bring him in and we'll tube him."

"Tube him?"

"Force a tube down his throat and pump liquid food directly into his stomach."

I looked at Caesar. Even skinny and lying by the door he seemed to block out the light in the room. He was civil enough when we petted him but he mostly ignored us and would pointedly push us out of the way when we came between him and the door. I didn't see how it would be possible to force him to do anything.

It was, in the end, nearly six full days before he came around. I genuinely feared for his life and had decided that if he didn't eat by the morning of the sixth day I would take him in to be force-fed.

The change came at six in the morning on the sixth day. I was sound asleep — actually close to comatose, as I'd been working on a construction crew pouring cement forms for basements and the work was killing me — and found myself suddenly lying on my side with my eyes open. I didn't remember waking up, but my eyes were open and I was staring directly into the slobbery muzzle of Caesar.

I closed my eyes — lost in sleep for a moment, I did not remember getting the dog — and kept them closed. It was no good. A tongue that seemed to be a foot wide and three feet long slathered spit up the middle of my face and I sat bolt upright and swore.

"Woof."

It was not loud but it was perfect — an exact *woof* — and he looked directly into my eyes when he made the sound. It was so pointed, so decisive and focused, I knew exactly what he wanted.

"What was that?" my wife asked without opening her eyes — indeed, she could talk without awakening.

"The dog," I said, "is ready to eat."

I rose and made my way to the kitchen, the Great Beast padding along behind me. On the floor were three dishes. One had held canned dog food, a second dry dog food and the third water. They were all empty, licked shiny, and I took the sack of dry food down and filled one of the bowls.

He looked at it, then at me.

"Was I wrong?" I said. "Aren't you hungry?"

He looked at the refrigerator, at the door handle.

"Something in there?"

I swear I saw him nod.

I opened the door and he slid his big head past my leg and studied the shelves for a moment before selecting a leftover chicken, which he swallowed virtually whole, then a cold beef sandwich I'd made for lunch — gone in a bite — and half a lemon meringue pie, before I could catch his collar and pull him back.

"Sit down . . ."

He sat — taking a few seconds to work his bony tail down — and looked at me and belched.

"You're welcome. Do you have to go outside?"

He jumped up and put his paws on my shoulders — his weight compressed my legs a full inch — and then made for the door.

I was in a bit of a dilemma. We lived in the mountains with a great deal of wild country around. The owner had said nothing about whether or not Caesar would run away, but he'd only been with us five nights and I wasn't sure he'd stay. I took his leash and hooked it to his collar and reached for the knob.

I would, I thought, hold him while

he did his business (a phrase I've always thought oddly appropriate).

We did not have neighbors within a quarter of a mile so I threw on a pair of sandals sitting by the door, hitched up my boxer shorts — all I was wearing — and opened the door.

I should add here that Caesar's collar was stout nylon and that the leash — which was about six feet long — had a forged-steel snap and was made from woven synthetic braid that would withstand a six-thousand-pound test and that I twisted the loop of the leash tightly around my wrist.

I think — little of it is clear in my memory — I *think* I had the door open an inch before everything went crazy. Later I would piece it together and come up with some of the details — a time-flow of the events leading up to the disaster.

I cracked the door. Caesar got his nose into the opening. He slammed through the door, taking the screen door off its hinges, and headed down the three steps to the gravel drive and across the drive, where I believe he had every intention of stopping to go to the bathroom. For a moment I came close to keeping up but then I lost a sandal — I thought of it later as blowing a tire — and from then on more or less dragged in back of him screaming obscenities and yelling at him to stop. And I think he had every thought to stop, as I said, but my wife's cat, a big tom named Arnie that had been off for days looking for a mate, chose that moment to return home. Arnie, of course, had no knowledge that we'd acquired a dog, not just a dog but a house of a dog, a dog to strike terror into a full-size lion, let alone a ten-pound house cat.

The effect was immediate. Arnie was a survivor and when he saw Caesar he did what he was best at — he turned and ran. Not up a tree, as one would suppose, but across the road and along a ditch. With a satisfied growl that sounded like thunder, Caesar gave chase.

My tripping feet had nearly caught up with him — I remember the heel of my one sandal slapping so fast it sounded like a motor running — and I was reaching to shorten the leash when Caesar went after Arnie, and I never quite caught up again.

We went through the neighbor's yard at what felt like twenty miles an hour — cat, bounding dog and dragging, underwear-clad human yelling in monosyllabic shrieks. My neighbor was standing in his garage and waved — he may have thought I was waving.

By this time I was just trying to stay alive and couldn't have cared less if Caesar got loose. Indeed I *wanted* him to get loose. But the leash loop was tight around my wrist. I found to my horror that I was along for the ride, and what a ride it was! We went through three more yards and the back of a bike rental shop along the road and finally slammed into the back doorway of a small cafe where, I learned later, Arnie sometimes went to beg his meals.

Arnie disappeared into the kitchen. Caesar tried to follow him and would have made it except that I became jammed in the door opening and even he could not pull me free.

There was a large woman there holding a very impressive cast-iron frying pan and she looked at me as she might look at a cockroach — looked directly at my head and then at the frying pan, which she hefted professionally. "Who are you?"

"I'm with him," I said, pointing at Caesar while trying to cover my body. My shorts were in tatters and my feet were badly scraped.

"It's wrong to chase cats," she said.

"I'm sorry," I said, and I meant it. Perhaps more than any time in my life I meant it.

"Go away." She pointed to the door with her frying pan. "And take your dog with you."

And so Caesar entered my life.

He became many things to us — friend, entertainer, horror show — but he was never, never boring and his life comes back now in a montage of memories.

There was the Halloween when he greeted a little boy who came to the door in a werewolf costume. There was one moment, priceless, when the two eyed each other, hairy monster-mask to Great Dane muzzle, at exactly the same height. I'm not certain what the little boy expected but he didn't quail — he leaned forward and growled. I'm not sure what Caesar had expected either but it certainly wasn't an angry werewolf. He made a sound like a train in a tunnel and disappeared into a dark corner of the bedroom closet and would not come out until all the little people stopped coming and the doorbell quit ringing. And it might be noted here that he had a remarkable memory. Every one of the seven years that he was with us, when the first trick-or-treater came to the door on Halloween, no matter the costume, Caesar went into the bedroom closet, pulled a housecoat over his eyes and would not come out until it was over. He had great heart, but courage against monsters wasn't in him.

Then there was the time I was playing "get the kitty" with him. Arnie wasn't there — usually he was off eating or trying to get married — and I would run around the house yelling at Caesar, "Get the kitty, get the kitty!" He would lope with me, jumping over furniture and knocking down tables (for obvious reasons I usually played this game only when my wife wasn't there), and I would run and yell and yell until he was so excited he would tear around the house by himself. (I know, I know, but it must be remembered we had no television or other forms of home entertainment.) If it worked well enough I could go and pour a cup of coffee and drink it while Caesar kept galloping, looking for the mystery kitty.

On this one morning I had done it particularly well and he was crazy with excitement, running up and down the stairs, spraying spit (we often had gobbets on the ceilings when he shook his head), bounding through the air with great glee, and just then, at the height of his crazed romp, just then the front doorbell buzzed and without thinking I opened it to see a package-delivery man standing there with a box in his arms.

Caesar went *over* me, through the screen and into the guy at shoulder height. He didn't bite, didn't actually hurt the man at all. In fact when the man was down on his back Caesar licked his face — an experience which I think could be duplicated by sticking your head in a car wash — but the effects were the same as if he'd attacked. The package went up in the air and crashed to the ground with a sound of breaking crockery (it had been a family heirloom vase sent by an aunt — and *had been* would be the correct words). The delivery man wet his pants and in a cloud of dog spit and dust clawed his way free, ran back to the truck and was gone before

I knew exactly what had happened. Soon after, we received a polite note saying that that particular company would no longer deliver packages to us.

Caesar never became angry. I never saw him fight or be aggressive to another dog, and while he loved to chase cats, Arnie particularly, when the day was done I would frequently find Arnie curled up on Caesar's back by the stove, the two of them sound asleep. But Caesar would get excited and forget himself when there was food involved, particularly when the food was a hot dog. I think he would have sold his soul for a hot dog. With mustard and relish. When we had hot dogs or went on a picnic he would sit and stare until somebody handed him a wiener and then he would hit like a gator. You had to throw it or he would get your whole hand in his mouth, up to the elbow.

I once was invited to a picnic and softball game in a small town nearby and since it was a nice day I thought it would be fun to bring Caesar. Had I thought a little more I would have remembered two things — that it was a picnic and they would have hot dogs and that Caesar *loved* to play ball — but then had I thought a little more I probably would not have owned Caesar in the first place.

I brought him out of the back of the truck and people came to see him — one young boy said he looked exactly like a four-legged dinosaur with hair — and after all the oohs and aahs at his size settled down, I left him in the truck with the windows open, told him forcefully, "Stay!" (ha!) and went off to see what was happening.

I had gone about forty yards, saying hello to people and picking up a can of soda, when I met an old friend and stopped to chat. I had my back to the parking area and I suppose heard some of the commotion that was starting but it didn't enter my mind until the man I was speaking to looked over my shoulder and said, "Isn't that Caesar?"

I turned and my heart froze. Caesar was standing next to a small girl — she couldn't have been four — and he towered over her. That wasn't so frightening as what the little girl was doing. She had taken a bite off a hot dog and was holding the remainder out to Caesar.

Images of destruction roared through my mind. He had truly enormous jaws (I could fit my head inside his mouth) and he snapped at his food violently, especially hot dogs. It was too far for me to run in time and I yelled but it was too late by ages and I wanted to close my eyes but didn't dare and as I watched, Caesar incredibly, with the gentleness of a baby lamb, reached delicately forward and took the hot dog from the girl. He swallowed it in one bite, then licked her face and moved on — though I was calling him — looking for the next child.

They loved him. Kids came from all corners and fed him hot dog after hot dog and he was as careful and gentle as he'd been with the little girl. By this time he had the attention of the crowd and everybody loved him so much I thought they were going to riot when I tried to put him back in the truck.

I let him out when the game started, and he went to work in the outfield. He would sit around center field, in back of the outfielders, and watch the batter. If the ball came long or went between the outfielders he would grab it and run to the nearest player and drop it. I know of two grounders he shagged to stop a double — I hit both of them and was held at first both times because Caesar stopped the ball when it slithered past both infielders and outfielders.

He loved the game and loved the day and when the afternoon was done we went back to the truck and a little girl came running up to me and held out a piece of paper.

Drawn on it in crayon was a picture of a dog, a big dog, with a yellow sun in back of him and stick figures hitting at balls, and scrawled across the bottom was:

WE LOVE YOU SEEZER.

He is gone now, gone some years from a combination of dysplasia and cancer that was impossible to cure or fix but I still have the drawing in a box somewhere. It shows up from time to time when I am moving or straightening things, and I think of him and the perfect summer afternoon when we ate hot dogs and played ball and made some new friends.

FRED AND PIG

Fred came to me in a small cardboard box filled with wood chips.

I had been in a bookstore in Bemidji, Minnesota, looking for a book on pickling fish. I love to eat pickled herring and had access to a large supply of small northern pike.

It was in this uncomplicated frame of mind that I met Fred.

I was at the curb when a small boy came up to me holding an old detergent box.

"Hey, mister," he said with the air of a con man, "you want to buy a puppy?"

"Buy?" I stopped and peered into the box. There was nothing but a pile of wood shavings. "What puppy?"

"He's in there, down in the wood. Dig him out."

I dug around in the shavings until my fingers hit the soft fur. There was a moment's hesitation, then a small growl; then a set of needle-sharp teeth ripped into the soft tip of my finger. "He bit me!"

The boy nodded. "He's half Lab and half something that came into the yard one night. Dad said he'd make a great watchdog."

I studied the boy. He was short, with frank blue eyes and golden blond hair. He didn't look like a con man.

"Let me get this straight. You want me to buy a puppy I can't see, that bites me, and you aren't sure who the father is?"

He thought a moment, then nodded. "Yep. He's a good watchdog. Look how he defends that box."

Just for the record, I was going to say no, but I looked down and a small black head appeared, with two floppy ears, a black button nose, two dark brown eyes and a little mouth that smiled at me. I know some people think dogs can't smile, but they can, and he did. I was sunk. I've always been a sucker for puppies. I can't get out of a dog pound without a dog, especially a cute one like Fred.

"How much?" I asked.

The truth was, it was silly to buy a puppy — you could go to any mall or shopping center parking lot and find someone trying to give them away. Add to that the fact that I was terminally broke and it became doubly crazy.

"Fifty dollars," the boy said without smiling or batting an eye.

"For a mutt puppy?"

He looked at me, calculating. "How about five bucks?"

"Done."

I gave him the money and took the dog and box and wood shavings and put them on the floor of the cab of my old truck. I had just lost a friend to cancer. His name had been Fred and I thought it would be nice to hear his name now and then, so I looked down into the box while I drove and I said, "Your name is Fred."

At home I took the pup out of the box and into the house, where he promptly peed on the floor and tore a hole in a couch cushion, spilled trash all over the kitchen floor, ripped open two bags of beans and rice in the pantry, dismembered a doll that a neighbor's daughter had left, ate the laces and tongues out of four pairs of shoes (but only the left shoe of each pair), absolutely destroyed a vacuum cleaner somebody foolishly had left in the same closet as the shoes, and stuck my wife's cat, Matilda, almost permanently onto the ceiling.

This was in the first twenty minutes

Fred was in the house, while I was looking for my wife to tell her I had brought a puppy home.

Of all the dogs I have had, Fred was the closest to being actually nuclear in his capacity for destruction. None of it was done with evil intent. He was a wonderfully happy pup and adult dog — inventive and with a great sense of humor, more of which later — but he was also amazingly persistent. Once he started a project, he simply would not stop until it was done. I think nothing illustrates this better than what came to be known as the great wire war.

Fred grew, in spite of early attempts by Matilda the cat to disconnect his head from his body. As an adult dog he became rotund and only fourteen inches tall — I think he must have been a Labrador–Norwegian elk-hound cross — but his shortness did not extend to his thinking or his appetite. He was as devoted to eating as he was to finding things to destroy. This fact led to the war.

We lived close to the land then, with four gardens and a wood-heated cabin in the forest where we canned and preserved our own food. This included raising a pig for ham and bacon. Because we didn't wish to become too attached to the meat supply, we simply called it Pig. (This didn't work, of course, and we wound up with a nearly quarter-ton pet named Pig who lived to be a ripe old age and died with his head in the trough, eating potato peelings.)

Fred quickly found that he and the pig shared a basic drive — to eat —

and he took to hitting the pig trough in search of goodies. This often proved marvelously fruitful. I had a friend who owned a supermarket and we obtained all his dated food for the pig. I once came home with a dozen angel food cakes, forty pints of whipping cream and fifty pints of strawberries. I dumped all this in the trough and watched Fred and the pig put their heads under, looking for berries and bits of cake and snorting bubbles of cream as they hunted.

Soon Fred became fat and spent most of his time with Pig. He would sleep and cuddle next to Pig at night, and during the day we almost always found them together.

The problem started when Pig looked over one day and saw the garden. Pigs are very smart — as smart as dogs and many people I have met — and no doubt deduced that if old food is good, fresh food must be better. By this time he weighed over two hundred pounds and was built like a tank, and like a tank he simply walked through the garden fence and started eating.

He ate most of a row of new red potatoes, burrowing the plants up with his nose, before I caught him and herded him back. After that no fence could hold him. He went under, over and around whatever I tried to build and was fast wrecking the whole garden. One day I was talking to an old farmer neighbor, who thought I was crazy not to just kill Pig and eat him, but if I wasn't going to kill the pig, he said, I should get an electric fence. I, of course, knew of electric fences — I had once talked my cousin into peeing on one — but they had slipped my mind.

"Get the kind that burns off weeds when they touch it. They're the strongest," the farmer added.

It took an afternoon to buy a fence and hook it up, during which time we lost half a dozen tomato plants and another row of potatoes.

The fence worked better than I had expected. I strung the wire around Pig's pen, then stood back and watched while Pig ambled close and took a snap in his ear. He never tried it again. I remember actually thinking that my troubles were over.

I had forgotten Fred.

I happened to be in the yard when the battle started and saw the whole thing. Fred knew nothing of electric fences. He was out tending the boundaries and, no doubt feeling a little peckish, decided to drop in on his old friend Pig for lunch.

The wire caught him exactly across the top of his head and dropped him as if he'd been hit by a stone. He was on his feet at once, his hair up, his teeth bared. There was no doubt who his enemy was. The wire. He shook his head, dug his feet in and lunged, grabbing at the thing with an iron-jawed death grip.

The result was spectacular. The voltage hit his wet mouth like a sledge and stiffened him like a poker. He snarled, growling deeper, and tried to hang on, but the jolt was too powerful and slammed him back and down on his rump.

Any other dog would have stopped.

Not Fred. He shook all over, looked at the twisted and bent wire, gave a ferocious bellow and attacked again. This time he must have really been hammered. He slammed back and forth and his hair stood on end until his tail looked like a black bottle-brush, but he would not let go. I ran to help him, worried that the electricity would kill him. Though his eyes had rolled back, with only the white showing, he had the wire clamped in his teeth in a vise grip and was slashing his head back and forth.

Just as I got there the wire snapped, disconnecting the circuit. Fred stood there, his hair still on end and his chest heaving. Then he spit the wire out, growled at it and walked away, still looking like a bottle-brush but with a great deal of dignity.

In the great wire war, only I was the loser. Pig continued to eat well and stayed happy. I reconnected the wire to hold him in.

Fred did not want to do battle again and stopped visiting Pig. But one morning I looked into the garden and saw him walking casually through the tomato patch, picking and eating only the good, ripe, full tomatoes. Fred had won.

QUINCY

Wild Dog of the Alaskan North

He did not *look* like a dog that ought to be named White Fang and come from a Jack London story. Indeed, he did not look like much of a dog at all. When I first saw Quincy he looked like a dust mop that had been dropped in grease and rolled in old coffee grounds.

It was, in the long line of dogs that have come into my life, one of the few times I had misgivings about taking on a new dog.

But sometimes joy comes in convoluted ways, and the way Quincy came to me was so complicated it didn't seem possible.

Briefly (as I pieced it together later):

I had decided I could not live unless I ran the Iditarod. I lived in Minnesota and began acquiring sled dogs and training them for the run north. It seemed an impossible dream. I had no money, not even a vehicle, no dog team, no chance of getting to Alaska.

At the same time somebody — either a fool or somebody truly evil and demented — left Quincy at the side of a freeway going into Anchorage, Alaska. Considering that I later found he had no car sense at all, it's a miracle he wasn't run down at once. A truck came along being driven by a dog musher. He saw Quincy and stopped and picked him up.

Meanwhile the town of Bemidji, Minnesota — or a large portion of it — decided to help me run the Iditarod. They had potlucks and raffles, and many people sponsored me. One man gave me an old truck, another a battery. Yet another man gave me a tire. A woman stopped me on the street and handed me ten dollars. "For the dogs," she said. "Spend it on the dogs."

In Alaska, Quincy was taken to the home of the dog musher. The musher lived well back into the bush — thirty miles from the nearest neighbor. Thirty miles of rivers, swamps, wolverines, wolves and black and brown bears. Quincy promptly ran off. He was approximately nine inches high at the shoulder, had four-inch legs and a long tail, and his whole body, including the tail, was covered with ratty, curly hair.

In Bemidji, I was loaned and given dogs. One of them came to me by devious means. A family had a Siberian husky that their child loved, but the dog had killed just about every pet and squirrel, chipmunk and rabbit in the vicinity. The neighbors wanted the dog shot — several had threatened to shoot it themselves. The owner smuggled the dog to me to try on the team and told his child the dog had run off. The dog was a love and she could pull — or so I thought at the time — like a truck. I was glad to have her. (She was, incidentally, the only purebred dog — a registered Siberian husky — I had on the team. The man who came in dead last in the race had a team of purebred Siberian huskies.) I plugged her into the team and began training in earnest.

At the same time, Quincy journeyed through thirty miles of wolf-, wolverine- and bear-infested wilderness on four-inch legs — it's hard to believe he could even get through the swamp grass, let alone the forest and predators — and showed up on the doorstep of a single woman in the process of building a log cabin and living in the woods with her two children. The woman had no idea where Quincy had come from but she took him in and loved him, after a fashion. She'd wanted a dog for a long time, for the kids. Not a small dog but something large and friendly they could roughhouse with. She told a friend she really wanted a Siberian husky. But Quincy had come to her door and she took him in and was happy with him — until she found he had an obsession with getting into trash. At the same time, she built a loft in her cabin and found that she didn't quite have the expertise to lay up a set of steps and instead was using a ladder to go to bed at night.

The Bemidji man who gave me an old truck decided to take some time off and go with me to Alaska to help me keep the truck running and handle the dogs for me while I trained in the mountains there. This man is also an expert carpenter and believes, always, in helping people.

We drove to Alaska from Minnesota. It was a major undertaking to drag a trailer holding twenty dogs in back of a 1960 half-ton Chevy pickup, in December, through country so daunting that many people hesitate to drive it even in the summer. It took eight days, driving twenty-four hours a day, often in low gear at four miles an hour, just to get to the Alaska line, stopping every four hours to let the dogs out, at temperatures fifty below and colder.

Meanwhile Quincy was snuggling in the warm cabin with the woman and her children, now and then getting into the trash and scattering it about the house.

We arrived in Alaska and set up camp in the bush. Everybody within half a state came to call — mostly to check out our dogs — and often they would stay a day or two to wait out a blizzard.

I soon found the Siberian husky had a serious flaw. She pulled wonderfully well for thirty miles. Not thirty-one, not twenty-nine. Exactly thirty. At that point each day she would stop pulling and simply trot along. Since the race is over a thousand miles and it is necessary to run seventy or eighty miles a day, a thirty-mile-a-day dog wouldn't make it.

One day a man I consider the most repellent man I have ever met came to call — green snot had frozen in his mustache and he kept licking at it while he talked — and he mentioned that he knew a woman who was living alone with her children in the woods and was so sick of climbing a ladder to her loft that she had promised an Alaskan salmon dinner to anybody who could make a set of stairs. We had been eating nothing but camp food for weeks — boiled potatoes, fried potatoes, stewed potatoes with hamburger, hamburger, and hamburger, in that order.

It sounded like a good offer so I hooked up a sled, my carpenter friend jumped in and off we went. Because it was only thirty miles I thought it a good chance to let the better dogs rest and run the Siberian husky. I had stopped running her altogether because she couldn't keep up with the rest.

We came on the cabin in the bush in the dark — it was light only an hour and a half each day at that time of the year — and I picketed the dogs to a chain I'd brought for the purpose. By the time I went in, my friend had met everybody and was busy laying out the stairway.

Our hostess was as good as her word, and we had a wonderful salmon dinner. Quincy greeted everybody with wiggles — he was always wonderfully affectionate — and I scooped him into my lap and fed him scraps while I ate and the conversation (as always) turned to dogs.

"He's a good little guy," I said.

"He gets in the trash all the time," she said.

"Still, he's a great dog."

"I really wanted a Siberian husky but I can have only one dog . . ."

"Have I," I said, holding Quincy closer, "got a deal for you."

So we left with one less dog in the team and Quincy bundled in a sleeping bag (he had no guard hair and couldn't take the cold well), riding in the sled, eyes peering out at the dogs pulling, and barking and whining encouragement now and then in the dark. And I had a new dog in my life.

What a dog he was, what an incredible dog! Many animals, even dogs, are predictable. Say a certain thing, do a certain thing and they will respond a certain way.

Quincy always kept us hopping, just trying to keep up. During the race he stayed in camp and when my wife came for the race he immediately became *her* dog. He loved me, he would play with me, he would talk to me, he would consider me, but if she was around I simply ceased to exist.

We took him home. I warned my wife, "He'll get into the trash," but he never, not once in the nine years that he lived with us, not a single time did he get into the trash.

I told her, "He may run off." He never left her side. I told her, "He seems to be timid around other dogs." He trotted into the sled dog kennel as if he owned the place, walked right into the circle belonging to Big Mac — an enormous dog from the Yukon that loved to fight and had nearly eaten a sled dog once — and Big Mac wagged his tail and started playing like a puppy with Quincy. I told her, "He might not be the smartest dog we ever got," but with the possible exception of Josh, a Border collie that is now in my life, Quincy proved to be easily the smartest dog I have ever seen.

An example: He loved to ride in cars with the window open and catch the air by leaning out. When we got up to seventy it was too much and blew him half into the backseat. He quickly learned that the vent would provide the same effect and so he would sit and watch out the windshield and when he saw something interesting ahead — a dog, a cat, another animal — he would jump down to the floor and put his nose against the vent to smell them as we passed. If the smell bothered him he would jump up and bark just as we went by.

One time we stopped at a bank drive-through window and the teller handed me a small dog treat for Quincy. Quincy's quick eyes seemed to light up when I gave him the treat. A week went by before I went to town again — we often didn't get there for weeks — and then a week later I had to run in for something around lunchtime. Quincy jumped in the car, and as we approached the bank he saw it coming, jumped down and smelled the vent, then jumped back up and barked softly, just once, as we drove past. A block later there was a Dairy Queen and I thought, What the heck, I'll get us a treat. Big mistake. When I stopped at the speaker to order, Quincy looked out at the service window, then jumped down and took a whiff at the vent. I'm not sure what he smelled but it apparently agreed with him, and as I drove forward to pick up my order, Quincy left me.

He leaped from the vent in one motion, over my lap, through the car window and into the service window. With a small scrabble of his short back legs, he hung for a moment on the edge, and then he was inside. I heard some yelling, saw people running and jumped from the car and ran inside, afraid of what I'd find.

People were standing as if in a tableau: the boy in his Dairy Queen hat and customers staring at Quincy. He had jumped from the window to the counter and was happily licking a sundae sitting next to the cash register.

The mother lode, I thought. From the Alaskan bush to a Dairy Queen in

Minnesota — what a great span of time and luck he had.

His greatest moment was yet to come and it was one which would ensure a life of joy and leisure as long as he walked the earth.

We lived on the edge of the northern bush and were frequently visited by natives of that wilderness. Porcupines, skunks, wolves, foxes, bear, weasels — all came to visit, and many exacted tribute. The skunks, foxes and weasels made it virtually impossible to raise chickens and we stopped trying. We had four gardens and every year the raccoons and bears would wreak havoc with the corn. The gardens were critical to us as a food source since we had very little income, so we had arranged a precarious truce with our wild neighbors. As long as the animals didn't do too much damage we could live with their raids. I planted three times the corn we needed, twice the potatoes and four times the tomatoes, and any surplus the animals didn't get we gave to friends. (One year this process resulted in our having nearly fourteen hundred *pounds* of tomatoes.)

But there were rogues, some that took too much, some that were violent. The worst of these were the bears. Most of them were mellow, some less so, and when they became too aggressive I would shoot a high-powered rifle near them and scare them off. This worked for a long time but some of them became accustomed to the crack of the rifle and didn't run; they would ignore yelling or banging of pans, but even then we were hesitant to go to the next phase — destroying the bear. By law, we were allowed to if they destroyed property or threatened us, but I had a rule that if they didn't actually attack one of the sled dogs — frequently they ate with the dogs and didn't bother them — or a person I would not shoot them. Indeed, in all my years of running dogs I had to shoot only one bear.

But one particular bear was becoming a problem. It had been in the garden several times and although it ran when I fired warning shots it seemed to hesitate. I decided it would be good to watch it.

But when the problem bear came back I wasn't there. I was in the kitchen and my wife was working in the garden. Quincy, as always, was by her side and she was on her hands and knees weeding when she heard a strange *whoof*ing sound nearby and looked up to see the problem bear coming at her. There was no warning, no stance, no threat — it was down and moving toward her.

We had procedures. Do not make eye contact, get up, back away, and she did all these things. They did not work. It kept coming and was clearly going to attack, was attacking, when Quincy went for the bear like a fur-covered bullet.

It was a draw as to who was more astonished, the bear or my wife. Quincy launched himself from the ground, four-inch legs pumping, and caught the bear in the center of its chest. He grabbed a mouthful of fur and hung on, clinging like a burr.

Surprised, the bear stopped and tried to bite at Quincy but the dog was in too close. The bear started scraping with its front paws and my wife chose that moment to use all the good luck from the rest of her life. She rushed in, grabbed Quincy, pulled him off the bear and ran for the house. For some reason — shock, perhaps — the bear did not follow her, and Quincy, miraculously, was not injured. Later, at the vet's, we couldn't find a scratch on him, nor any internal injuries.

Quincy just passed on last year at the ripe old age (he was well on when we got him in Alaska) of eighteen or twenty years, as near as the doctor could figure. At the end he was blind and close to deaf but he could still smell, and to his last days he would stick his nose to the vent and tell us when we were coming up on the Dairy Queen, and he still would have jumped through the window if he had gotten a chance.

He should have been named White Fang.

JOSH

The Smartest Dog in the World

He sits now as I write this, watching me, waiting, his brown eyes soft but alert, full of love but without nonsense, his black-and-white coat shining in the New Mexico sun streaming through the window. He is old now — I think eighteen or twenty — and he is staid except when he feels like playing and he is full of a gentle honor that I will never come close to achieving.

Josh is the quintessential Border collie. In many circles that would be all that needed to be said — he has all the traits of Border collies. He is loving, thoughtful, wonderfully intelligent — frighteningly so at times — and completely and totally devoted to the person he views as his master.

And yet . . .

Somehow, in some way he is different. Perhaps that is true of all Border collies, that they really *are* different, that they key in to the person they are with, and since all people are different all Border collies are different. I recently gave a Border collie pup to a friend who lives in a city — contrary to popular belief, they do not need to run all the time — and the dog (she named him Maddux after the incredible pitcher for the Braves) has keyed in to her life to the point where he *has* to help her carry her mail, *has* to help her open envelopes, *has* to have coffee and a bagel each morning with her, *has* to be with her wherever she is in the house, *has* to greet people at the door. He monitors all the street activity and reports anything he thinks is odd and protects her from the evil monster that lives in the vacuum cleaner — and he's only a pup.

But there is more with Josh.

He is . . . real. No, more than that, he is a person. I do not think in my heart that he is a dog. When I am riding with him in my truck and he sits next to me looking out the window I can speak to him, say, "Look at that nice lawn," or "They have a sale on fence at the lumberyard," and he will look and sometimes (I swear) turn back to me and nod.

Once while driving to get a submarine sandwich I took my baseball cap off at a stoplight and jokingly put it on Josh with the bill backward and put a pair of sunglasses on him (I know — people shouldn't dress dogs but it was more a friend fooling around with a friend) and told him, "You look cool, man."

He looked at me and put his right front leg up on the ledge of the open window and kept the cap and glasses on (though he could have shaken them off easily) and really *did* look cool, caught in the moment, playacting with me, and when we pulled up to the drive-through window at the sub shop I said, "My friend and I would like a turkey sub." Josh looked over, through his shades, nodded and went back to looking out the window.

There are major stages that affect our lives. Enlisting in the army, marriage, success or failure at our careers — leaps forward or backward. Having Josh has had such an effect on me. He has, in wonderful ways, shaken my belief structures to the core and brought me to a level of understanding of other species that has been so profound it will last the rest of my life. Along with Cookie, Josh has changed me forever.

He came to me because he was a "naughty" dog. The woman who owned him had some pet ducks and

Josh herded them — as Border collies are wont to do — until he wore them out and one of them died. I had seen Josh earlier and thought he was a nice dog and jokingly said, "If you ever want to get rid of him let me know."

And so he arrived one day. He jumped out of the car, moved into the house and started — as near as I could figure it — to study me.

It was very disconcerting at first. I would catch him at odd times, at all times, watching me, watching every move, studying everything I did — or said.

He once saw me hurry to get to a phone because I was expecting an important call and after that wherever he was when the phone rang he would run to it and wait until it was answered.

He saw me, just once, put on a Stetson, go outside to saddle my mare and head out to ride fence. The next time I put the Stetson on he ran to the front door, slammed open the screen, loped to the corral, cut my mare away from the other horses and brought her to the gate, holding her there until I came to saddle her.

Once every nine days we get the flow of water in the communal irrigation ditch. The process is rather involved. I must walk to the head of the ditch and open the valve, then move ahead of the water as it pours down the ditch and clean out brush and debris with a rake. When the water gets to the smaller ditches that run to the apple trees or the pecans, these side ditches must be fully cleared of leaves and grass before the water can run on to the next side ditch, and so on for seven side ditches.

Josh accompanied me the first time and watched what I did. Just once. The next time I went he actually tried to help open the valve with his teeth — cranking the steel-handled wheel — and when the water started he ran frantically ahead of it, scrabbling with his feet and claws to clean out the brush and junk. He went to each side ditch, one after the other, to clear it out carefully and make certain the water was running correctly, then on to the next ditch. I stood leaning on the rake, my mouth hanging open. Josh had actually figured it out quicker than I had the first time. And when the last ditch was running and too much water was coming — flooding out over the end — Josh studied the situation for a moment, then dug a cross ditch that made the water circle back into the ditch.

So many similar things happened that I thought maybe he was some kind of odd case — not normal even for a Border collie. When we had people to the house he would try to get them all in one room, gently pushing them into a group with his shoulder — it would take him thirty minutes to move a small child from one room to another — and I thought it might be some perversion of the herding instinct. But it wasn't that so much as it was the fact that he simply wanted to see them all, watch over them. When somebody went to the kitchen or the bathroom he would accompany them if possible and watch over them until they came back, and then when it was time to leave he would escort each of them to their car, wait until they were gone and then escort the next one. He was, I believe now, merely being polite — trying to be a good host. Understand that I've had hundreds of dogs and loved them and, I hope, been loved by them, and I've been in God knows how many different kinds of situations with them, but I had never, ever seen anything like Josh. I half expected him to come out of the kitchen with a tray saying, "Canapés, anyone?"

I thought I should learn if he really was unique and so one summer four years ago I went to the international Border collie field trials in Sheridan, Wyoming.

It was absolutely astonishing. Had I

not seen it myself, had somebody written of it in a book, as I am trying to do now, I do not think I would have believed it.

A man would stand in one place and send a dog out half a mile to where some sheep stood, and following whistles, and sometimes gestures, the dog would bring the sheep back through gates, around in a circle by the man, then into a small holding pen — all without making a sound and without ever biting (called "gripping") or touching a sheep, using only eye contact and body language. That was incredible enough, but another thing was in some ways more incredible, and that was the behavior of the dogs themselves.

I have been to sled dog races where there were hundreds of dogs and if two or three of them got loose — which inevitably happened — there would be an uproar — barking and snarling and most often fights or attempted fights. The dogs had to be kept tethered and watched closely.

All the collies were loose. There were hundreds of them, and I never saw a leash or a pen. Nor did I ever see a fight or even hear a bark. It was a hot summer day and a large stock tank had been brought in and filled with water. As each dog finished his work he (or she) would go to the tank, jump in, submerge until only eyes and nose showed, and stay that way for a few minutes, until he had cooled down. Then he would jump out and catch up with his master, who was by then a hundred yards off drinking lemonade and talking with other dog owners, and he would stop and sit by his owner's leg and look up and listen to the conversation.

And they do listen. All the time. To *all* talk.

Josh has come to know dozens of individual words. To name just a few: *horse, mare, cow, truck, car, walk, run, bike, Dairy Queen* (also the initials *DQ*), *deer, cat, dog, sub sandwich, turkey sandwich, hamburger, pancake* (he *loves* blueberry pancakes), *gun* (he hates guns), *thunder* (the only thing I've ever seen truly terrify him — he comes to sit in my lap when it thunders), *fence, elk, moose, bear, blabber* (a kind of candy I sometimes share with him), *telephone, bug* (he sometimes studies bugs as they crawl along the ground — never bothers them, just walks along studying them), *baby, snake* (he respects rattlers but doesn't fear them), *rabbit, flyswatter* (he leaves the room if you say the word — I do not know why), and several more Anglo-Saxon expressions he's heard me use when required, such as *Get the —————— horse off my —————— leg before I —————— bleed to ——————— death!*

And he knows them out of context. I have often been having a conversation on the phone about, say, the weather, and inserted a word: "I think it's going to be cow a nice day," with no emphasis on the word at all. Wherever he is in the house he will rise, even if sleeping, and come in and look at me or wait by the door. More, he listens to everybody all the time. If several people are in a conversation and just one of them says a word —

again, just in a normal tone — Josh will come in and look up and wait. It can be very disconcerting if you're having a conversation in which you might use one of the words a lot. I had a sick horse and called the vet and used the word *horse* several times in the conversation, and each time Josh went to the door and tried to get out, finally coming back to me and biting me on the leg to get my attention, gently at first and then harder when that didn't work and finally — he's learned this is particularly effective — grabbing my kneecap and exerting enough pressure to make me utter a profanity. Usually I react then and do what he wants.

He has wonderful limits. He will do anything I ask and many things I tell him to do, unless he thinks they are too stupid or repetitive or boring. He will retrieve, for instance, and do it with great élan, leaping to fetch things thrown in water, over land, in brush, far away or near — but only five times. If you throw the ball the sixth time he will get it, look at you, then leave with the ball in his mouth and never bring it back. He hides it. If you want to play again the next day you must buy another ball. I was recently moving some old hay bales and when I lifted one that had been near the back corner of the storage area, I found eleven tennis balls and four Superballs and a professional retriever's canvas dummy bird. Josh had hidden them all when he thought the game had become too stupid.

Josh is wonderfully facile and will humor me and learn dog tricks — up to a point. I taught him to sit up and hold a cookie on his nose until I commanded him to flip it in the air and catch it. He loves cookies and he learned the trick in less than ten minutes. And he did it five times. The sixth time, he looked at me over the cookie on his nose as if I was completely insane, then lowered his nose, let the cookie drop on the floor and walked away, and we don't do the cookie trick anymore. Not unless I want to sit up on *my* hind end and put the cookie on *my* nose and flip *my* head up and catch the cookie, we don't.

Living with Josh is a never-ending lesson in how we can never truly catch up with somebody who is smarter than we are. One day I was moving some sacks of feed and as I got down to the last sack I saw a rat run in back of it and hide. There was nowhere for it to go and Josh was there so I looked at him and grabbed the bag and told him, "Get ready — get ready now. There's something there. Are you ready? Ready?" until he was excited enough to jump out of his skin, and then I moved the sack and the rat made its break. Josh grabbed it without hesitation but didn't kill it. Holding it in his mouth, he looked up at me in total disgust as if to say, "You fool — I've got a *rat* in my mouth," then turned sideways and spit it out — he distinctly made the sound *ptui* as he did it — and then walked away from me.

It wasn't finished either. The next morning in my boot there was a dead gopher. It had been dead for some time and smelled as rotten as old, long-dead gophers dragged off the highway can smell, and I shook it out in the trash and thought, Fine, message received.

I discovered one day by accident that Josh is wonderfully, wildly ticklish on his ribs and sometimes when he seems to be getting too serious about things — say two or three dozen times a day — I will grab him and flip him on his back and tickle his ribs while he woof-laughs and wiggles and air-snaps his fangs, always just missing my hands and arms. It's a ritual we have both come to love and sometimes when he is feeling a bit glum he will come up to me and flop over and invite me to tickle him.

Life is not always up and once I had about a three-day run of luck that was all bad and I never smiled. Some complete jerk shot a new Border collie pup I had gotten for Josh to train. (The pup's name is Walt and he has more or less recovered but it was so stupid and ridiculously violent — the idiot just shot him to see if his damn gun worked — that it made me sick of the whole human race for a time.) I also had a friend die and couldn't get to his funeral in time . . . just misery. At the height of this I was sitting in an old easy chair with my legs stretched out thinking dark thoughts and Josh came up in front of me and sat, studying me for a full minute, his eyes clear and calm. Then he seemed to shrug, turned around so he had his back to me, straddled my boot, then backed up my leg until his teeth were even with my foot. I had never seen him do anything like it and thought he might be going crazy when suddenly he reached down, grabbed my boot and with a mighty lunge jerked me completely out of the chair on my butt and then jumped on me and pretended to be biting my ribs, back and forth, tickling me.

Enough of the blues, by God — it was time to laugh. And I did, rolling on the floor with him, and we tickled each other until we knocked over an end table and had to quit.

Then — his job completed; I was cheerful again — he was sober once more, sitting quietly, listening in case I said a word he needed to respond to, watching me, anticipating where I would go, what I would do, out ahead of me like an infantry point — no, like a spirit, like an extension of my mind.

If possible Josh is always with me. Sleeping, awake — I even took him on an author tour once — he is always, always there. When I ran sled dogs he tried to go, put himself in the team, and when I threw a harness on him he pulled wonderfully. But he was too . . . too refined for that work. The sled dogs are wonderful but they are primitive, basic, grandly pre-historic and animal. It was like putting a neurosurgeon in the middle of a professional hockey team and expecting him to be able to function, so I took Josh out.

A last picture of Josh:
I am riding a horse, leading a pack-horse up into the Bighorn Mountains out of Story, Wyoming. All mountains are beautiful but there is something

about the Bighorns that is particularly wonderful, and I have trained one horse to carry a pack so I can head up and spend some time alone wandering, looking.

Well, not alone. The horses are there, of course, and they provide some company, and there is Josh.

When I left the sled dogs because of my heart and went to horses, Josh fit right in, as I should have known he would. At first he trailed along on rides — just at first; then he saw that most of the problems with horses come from the front: deer, snakes, moose, bear, mountain lions — anything that would scare the horses and make them shy and throw me (which happened several times). Then he moved of his own volition to the front.

Josh knew his job was to lead always, to handle problems, to run ahead, out there about forty to fifty yards, trotting up the trail leading bear off, turning moose and elk away, dodging around snakes; doing all this day in, day out, until the mare knew him, understood what he was doing and trusted him. I think in a way the mare came to love Josh, because she would sometimes come up to him when he wasn't looking and nuzzle the back of his head as if petting him.

But that one picture of him is always clear in my mind. Head and tail down slightly, body relaxed but still somehow tensed and ready. The Bighorn Mountains wild across the sky above us and Josh trotting up the trail ahead, looking back at me on the horse, to make sure I'm coming.